Boundary Disruption

short-form poems

Boundary Disruption

short-form poems

by
Erin Castaldi

Encircle Publications, LLC
Farmington, Maine USA

Boundary Disruption ©2022 Erin Castaldi

Paperback ISBN-13: 978-1-64599-367-4
eBook ISBN-13: 978-1-64599-368-1

All rights reserved. No part of this book may be reproduced in any form by any mechanical or electronic means including storage and retrieval systems without express written permission in writing from the publisher. Brief passages may be quoted in review. Rights to individual poems remain with the author.

Editor: Cynthia Brackett-Vincent
Book and book cover design: Eddie Vincent/ENC Graphics Services
Cover Image: Erin Castaldi

Sign up for Encircle Publications newsletter and specials
http://eepurl.com/cs8taP

Mail Orders, Author Inquiries:
Encircle Publications
PO Box 187
Farmington, ME USA 04938

Online orders:
encirclepub.com

I dedicate this book to my husband of fifteen years. He has continuously shown me bountiful kindness and understanding. I am forever grateful for his insight and how he loves me.

Publication Credits

A tornado of gnats;	*Cicada's Cry*, Summer 2018
Between us;	*Wild Plum* Haiku Contest 3rd Place Winner
Both of us;	*Blithe Spirit*, 2020 Issue 30.3
Caught;	*ChaNoKeburi*, Autumn 2019
Crack of thunder;	*Akitsu Quarterly*, Winter 2020/21
Dry lake bed;	*Poetry Pea Podcast*, September 2020
First touch;	International Haiku Competition, Honorable Mention 2020
In the silence;	*Akitsu Quarterly*, Summer 2019
Japanese apricot;	*#FemKuMag*, May 2019
Mangled thoughts;	World Haiku Series 2020
Rain again;	*The Heron's Nest*, June 2020
Tree branches;	*Indigenous Media Anthology*, haiga 2020
Wild bitter;	*Akitsu Quarterly*, Autumn 2020
Wilting wildflowers;	*Blithe Spirit*, Summer 2020, Issue 30.3

crack of thunder
a tumble of pines
            rolls out to sea

tree branches
        thick with plump buds
we arrive
        in a new place
social distance

talking
at me not to me
      quarantine

in the silence
       between sounds
lava flow

Japanese apricot
the walls we build
        around ourselves

    mask-less
he wanders in
    out of my mind

     caught
        between rainbows
warm drizzle

           sour peach pit
only these two
                gold rings

presses 'send'
                immediately rethinking
this route home

dry lake bed
the rainy season's
    unresistant path

                              untangling the twisted
     knots of matrimony
                    snow-blind

between us
        a rock and moss
d r i f t i n g clouds

wilting wildflowers
      remembering the way
             we were

a tornado of gnats
      redirects
            the sparrow's flight

first touch
        the soft flesh
persimmon harvest

wild bitter
the heart of Spring's
        first crocus

slow talker
      the smooth pour
           melted caramel

rain again
           I read myself
                      to sleep

    verge of tears
the unrepentant sun
            in my eyes

lies awake
          mulling
                    greener grass

petals plucked
        near you, are you
in Pittsburg mist
        the reddest leaf
a simple token

       he tries
loving me...
               blustery winds

mangled thoughts
        of myself—
                white water rapids

                                        fabulist
                        a teller of half truths
        shifting seasons

accepting
>   the unacceptable
>   spring mud

                    both of us
        knowing who's at fault
                    falling Dogwood petals

sixth sense
           faith in the peony
                            to bloom
                  again

About the Author

Erin Castaldi's work has appeared in many journals including *Akitsu Quarterly, Alien Buddha Press, Asahi Haikuist, Blithe Spirit, ChaNoKeburi, Chrysanthemum, Failed Haiku, #FemKuMag, Frogpond, Hedgerow, Heron's Nest, Japan Society, Mayfly, Modern Haiku, Presence, Prune Juice, tsuri-doro,* and *Wales Haiku Journal,* as well as at least a dozen anthologies.

Winning third place in the Wild Plum Haiku Contest 2019, she was nominated twice for a Touchstone Award for a single haiku in 2019 and 2021 and received an honorable mention in the Green Pencil Haiku Contest 2018 and another at the Vancouver Cherry Blossom Haiku Contest 2020, as well as Honorable Mention in the Kaji Aso Studio International Haiku Contest 2021. Erin has had work translated into Japanese, Croatian, Romanian, Italian, German and Chinese.

Erin was previously the social media manager for The Haiku Society of America (HSA) and until very recently, secretary for the United Haiku and Tanka Society. She edited the Haiku Society of America's Member's Anthology 2021. In a former life, Erin was employed as a surveillance officer in a large casino in Atlantic City and was for a time, an Emergency Medical Technician (EMT).

She operates a small business that is thriving nationally. Erin lives and writes in New Jersey where she writes about nature in all her splendid forms, and where she is currently Poet Laureate of the city of Somers Point.

www.ingramcontent.com/pod-product-compliance
Lightning Source LLC
Chambersburg PA
CBHW060413080526
44583CB00012B/557